Cows

Children Book of Fun Facts & Amazing Photos on Animals in Nature - A Wonderful Cows Book for Kids aged 3-7

By

Ina Felix

Ina Felix

Do you want to know about cows?

All cows go MOO MOO MOO!

It is not just a sound with an O at the end.

It is how they talk with their other cow friends.

Cows can always be found in groups.

A group of cows is called a herd. That is the name of their troop.

A calf is what you call a baby cow.

There are one billion cows in the world right now!

One billion cows is a lot of milk.

Oh yes, cows produce our favorite drink.

They can give you six gallons of milk every day.

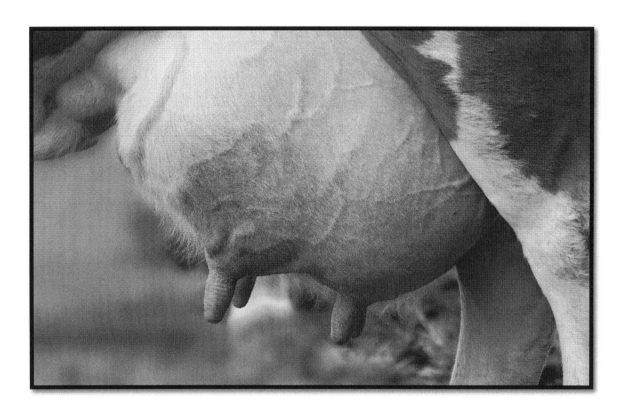

So drink lots of it, as your mother would say!

And from milk comes butter, and cheese and more.

Ice cream and other dairy products galore.

Did you know that cows are called herbivores?

That means they eat only grass and plants, nothing more.

Cows drink thirty five gallons of water a day.

One bathtub full of water, to wash down all that hay.

Cows have black-and-white or brown-and-white spots.

Whatever their colors would be, be sure to love them lots!

I hope you had fun learning about my family.

Thank you.